WOUNDS FROM IRAQ

Wounds from Iraq

poems by
Ahmad Al-Khatat

Poetic Justice Books & Arts
Port Saint Lucie, Florida

©2019 Ahmad Al-Khatat

book design and layout: SpiNDec, Port Saint Lucie, FL
cover design: Manon Seck

All rights reserved.

No part of this book may be used or reproduced in any manner whatsoever without written permission except in the case of brief quotations embodied in critical articles and reviews. Members of educational institutions and organizations wishing to photocopy any of the work for classroom use, or authors, artists and publishers who would like to obtain permission for any material in the work, should contact the publisher.

Published by Poetic Justice Books
Port Saint Lucie, Florida
www.poeticjusticebooks.com

isbn: 978-1-950433-11-7

FIRST EDITION
10 9 8 7 6 5 4 3 2 1

Wounds from Iraq

Unspoken Language 3
Everything Is Miserable Here 4
The Cost of Cigarettes 5
In a Random Street in Baghdad 6
Iraqi Soil 7
My Colourful Sorrows in Iraq 8
Wounds from Iraq 9
Death 10
At the Airport 11
The Baghdad Taxi 12
The Beautiful Dream of Baghdad 13
Grief and Palm Trees in Iraq 14
Iraq 15
Children of the Moon 16
The Theory of Death 18
Send My Salutations 19
The Broken Gates 20
Inside Peace 22
My Name Is Iraq 23
Flooding in Aleppo... 25
Lonely Again 27
Colourless Dream 28
The Crying Girl on the Border 30
Will the Gate of Mesopotamia Open for Us? 31
If Santa Clause Was In... 33
My Childhood 35
Water Versus Wine 36

Wounds from Iraq

Unspoken Language

Death is the only
unspoken language
in my country,
yet everybody
speaks it well

I don't know if
I should learn how
to speak it before I
die uneducated to
explain to God about my tears

Everything Is Miserable Here

Everything is miserable here
Nothing is clean or clear to
trust the hidden sidewalk

weak chickens in rusty cages
with less feathers on their skin
waiting to be slaughtered by the butcher

he's only fourteen years old
he smokes a cigarette in one hand
and use the other hand to sharpen his knife

the ones who sell vegetables are
even more dirty than wild-pigs
they scream as no one has ears to hear them

The cats and dogs walk on the streets
looking for anything to eat for the day
yet, some people are waiting to hurt them

Once the moon appears in the sky
I talk to the invisible stars with hope
that they will make my wishes come true

and wipe the rules of the tribes away
far away from the town, therefore the
sun arises far from another bloody revenge

The Cost of Cigarettes

nowhere else but in my country
every child, teen, and adult smokes
there is no age limit or strict rules

one pack of cigarettes cost forty cents
therefore, even the bigger and street-
children can offer the cost of death

some people have money to create
trouble against everything but doesn't
have money to stop inhaling cancer

some children work through blindfolded labor
with pay that is only affordable for a pack
of cigarettes, bills, and one can of beer

teenagers have lack of knowledge
about describing their views of the future
as they smoke and drink alcohol

Instead adults smoke until they die
as if it is the greatest way to say farewell to life
even after their death, they will dive in sorrows

In a Random Street in Baghdad

The first car
I was on the streets of Baghdad
the driver was playing a
radio station with a song
of my favorite artist

The name of the song was
"liar" and everything about you
is a lie, at that moment I felt
down and knew that my painting
of my homeland was not the same

I felt nostalgic for roses and flowers
I missed the sound of the voiceless joys
so much feelings I have and nothing was
seen but lightless streets accept the lonely moon
It is hidden from the scent of my sorrows

All I could remember of the city streets
Were the pictures of Martyrs beside
the leaders who damaged the rainbows
and the scent of the sinless wine to my thirst
even the people are wolves from the inside

Everything was rising in my dry veins
my depression became severe
my anxiety became a sharp knife
yet, my eyes were unable to cry about
my own misery, since my dreams weren't stable

Iraqi Soil

I saw an old man
He was around my
Father's age or
Maybe even older

he was crying
until I saw his son
Pouring Iraqi soil
on his bare flesh

Only because
He was getting
ready to die
slowly before the

Victory of the war...

My Colourful Sorrows in Iraq

I asked my life sorrows
why we are always together
he responds to me with;

because happiness will
never make your dreams
come true with beautiful colors

sorrows will be your only
friend until the cloud's
paint your flesh colorlessly

Wounds from Iraq

Wounds from Iraq
are growing continuously
with blood shed

Nobody forgives or
Watch's the time to
plant stars for the lightless day

I walk around mindlessly
as some want to talk with me
sharing kindness and ethics in sorrows

Pure Love is hidden by
The revenge of betrayal
everything is growing grey and dusty

The faces of healing
I don't see candles on
but bitter tears rolling down the sunshine

Death

In my country
everything is related
to death

I smell death
I swallow death
and I hear about hope
from the distance
of death

I see death
and I realize that
he is a harmless angel
collecting spirits
as he creates more
widows
and orphans
in the land of
death

At the Airport

Once the plane landed
I was really happy as
a bird flying away from
the chasers and snow falcon

I met with men
to stamp my passport
and were around my age
but was chewing gum like a cow

Baghdad in my fantasies was
cut down into pieces for the fire
and once I walked outside I
stepped on the unwelcoming soil

I was wondering how my days
will go by as my mind starts feeling
low as once my spirit was truly happy
to see my city in the colours of life

The Baghdad Taxi

The Baghdad Taxi driver
was a funny, outgoing,
one of his kind, religious,
talkative and quietly drunk

I asked about tourism in this place
and he took me to a dusty cemetery
with his pre-made tomb
by the cigarette butts

I asked about a coffee shop
he invited me to an escort show
with a cup of watery alcohol
that tasted like the sweat of fear

He has the skill
to be a professional racer
he drove with no fears from the
soldiers with their guns filled with courage

The last taxi driver I had
he could not drive me there
only because he just got a
call that death was secretly invited to his

comfort space

The Beautiful Dream of Baghdad

Since I was little
I used to wait for the end of the rain
to observe the details of the rainbow
to remember its colours and its magic

I drew the beautiful dream of Baghdad
hoping nobody would damage the colours
with the innocent laughter of children
as they play together under the sun

as I grow more grey hair,
the colours were becoming darker
Baghdad lost my touch and my footprints
And those children flew to heaven

I arrived in Baghdad and I thought
my paintbrush would create paintings
the rainbow appeared with Jesus tears
as if the Iraq was bleeding to death

People were smiling and I was wondering
if I should smile as I am already dying
I look at my canvas with lines in black and
red, it was the battle of death against grief

Grief and Palm Trees in Iraq

Grief in
Iraq
could be
everything,
a great religion
a damaged faith
a good holiday
a miserable widow
a heartbroken orphan
a wounded soldier

like a regular palm tree
in Iraq
It could be;
a dusty chair
a hungry plate
a forgotten table
a dirty shirt
a delicious fruit
a bottle of water

Iraq

They have said that Iraq
Is not the same as before
It is damaged and dangerous

I told my friends about my funeral
the same day I walked in the airport
and my father called the gravedigger

I inhaled the first breathe of Baghdad
my eyes were crying like autumn rain
as my coffin was turning into a black cloud

I was in a battle with life and death
until I heard the prayers of the widows
and the joys of orphans waiting for my arrival

I became stronger than my weak spirit
I heard my grandparents in the tombs as he
welcomed my father in paradise

I didn't see blood spots or blindfolded bullets
but I did see the dead flowers and roses, it was
then I realized that there is hope as it will rest and die in

Baghdad

Children of the Moon

Children of the moon
were innocent
but their parents were
greedy and selfish

they taught them nothing
of knowledge or practical
instead, they taught them
to be dirty beggars

their lives had been coloured
with the colour of dust and
confusion, they wore grief
beneath their innocent joy

their parents walked them to
the orphanage in the night
with the intention to sell them
to stain their hands black and dusty

they spent the nights awake
staring at the moon till sunlight
with tears wondering why
they have miserable lives

days come and nights go by
those children die for feeling
depressed at a young age
from questions without answers

from talking to the moon
about dreams that faded in the night
as their parents once broke their
hearts for a few paper bills
While I am smiling and recalling

My mother in the city...

The Theory of Death

We were the lucky ones
to live in a house filled with hope
my father was the General and
my mother was a housewife

but our neighbors were like
monsters and gods, they were
judging and shooting each other
as the echoes of souls were in grief

with seconds, houses were destroyed
and the bloody bodies flew to the sky
reaching the angels in paradise
instead of waiting in the dust of darkness

we survived until the last breath of war,
defenseless to walk away from the cemetery
my father once said, I do not like where this
is going, and died after he denied

the theory of death

Send My Salutations

My salutations to you, my country;
I am sending my salutes.
From my family to your family
I send my special salutations
I sacrifice my soul for my religion,
and I send my greetings.
I used to pray for love and peace.
My prayers are to none but my God,
and I send my salutations.

My greetings to my homeland,
the martyr, and I send my salutations.
My country's status will stay elevated,
and to it I send my salutes.
To my homeland I will return eagerly
and in peace. I will visit its grave;
Fluttering over it will be the pigeons
of peace. To my country,
whose peace has been slaughtered,

I send my salutations.

The Broken Gates

It has already been seventy three years and
The Holocaust still remains like yesterday
It has been years and years and slavery
Flew inside our miserable damaged arteries

Yet, nobody feels the brutality of the recent history
As today world disasters, are shown on Netflix
Even the brave man out there on a lonely island
died because he could not help the illegal immigrants
　from the wooden ships

Everyone remembers you for their benefit,
Kids cry for being taken away from their parents
Parents weep for seeing their children as strangers
They were adopted by other parents to have a better life

The cemetery is missing the young visitors nowadays
When most of those soldiers are buried somewhere else
Ladies stand by the flowers day and night with hope
They will return without a coffin, nor a single old picture

I feel today a season is like a season of stolen souls and
Not to bloom roses and plants in my backyard
My parents taught me not to walk with strangers
But now I feel I am the weakest to help others who
　needs my help

Shall I sleep in the spider's web for today and
Hear the orphan's tale of a bird with a broken wing

The water in the river dried out, the rocks cracked into Stones, and my heart beats by the broken gates of my homeland

Inside Peace

Inside peace
There, no peace talks
Inside peace
There is an orphan peeing in the bloody sea
and a virgin widow vomiting from a soldier's rape.

Inside peace
There is no peace makers
Inside peace
there is a homeless asking the world for peace
and a businessman who avoids paying to the charity

Inside peace
There is a good stranger
Inside peace
there is hunger and thirst on my enemy's face
Inside peace
there is a peaceful dove breaking his own wings

My Name Is Iraq

My name is Iraq
My age is a forgotten number
United Nations' numbered me
As an immigrant and a terrorist

My name is Iraq
My hobbies are to write about
What the world mostly ignores
Read with eyes closed with tears

My name is Iraq
My heart is a unique candle
It burns after a bloody explosion
It melts by the death of the innocent

My name is Iraq
My friends are volunteer heroes
Others have stabbed me painfully
Some drown me with bare hands

My name is Iraq
My family is always close together
Muslim and Christian's are life's destiny
Yazidism and Judaism are the brave

My name is Iraq
Dauntless from the death and curse
I raise men and death digs more graves
Children are blessed and grief brings them to heaven

My name is Iraq
My obsession is missing my old memories
My best interest is crying day and night
With nobody else to wipe my running tears

My name is Iraq
My face can gage without knowledge
But if I am sad then I could feel the clock
Tick tack with the speed of my heart beats

My name is Iraq
My actual voice is low, but never the echoes
Low to respect the widow's prayers to God
Also to hear orphans whispering to the angels

My name is Iraq
Dipped in the land of bullets and sorrowful
Still believe that the sun will shine beautifully
And the sky will be always stunning and blue

My name is Iraq
My ears will they hear the sound of the holidays
Without a spot of blood and moaning of spirits
And watch the moon with the stars clear in a

Iraqi angel from Baghdad and cuddle with me
And hold my hands with rings of being lovers
Nothing can stop us to live or die for in Mosul

Flooding in Aleppo...

The coming and the
Unborn history will
Turn blind eyes,
From the disaster of the
Flooding in Aleppo.

Daily floods everywhere,
Often death purpose,
Nightly dreams disappear,
Regularly flying spirits,
UN remains reticence.

Every single home,
Floods of tears,
From youthful and
Aged widows,
By photo albums.
On damage streets,
Flood of blood,
Of innocent angels,
From car bomb,
From flying rockets.

The blue sky
Becomes the clouds,
And rain warmly,
Peace birds fly,
To pray mercies.

Red in exile,
States as warning,
Red in Syria,
Assigned as death,
Leaders keep ignoring.

The green soil
Flood of skeletons,
From mass grave,
Of unknown fighters,
With white flags.

One dictator leader,
Smiles with fears,
Mothers still weep,
Tears flood hopes,
Tanks kill everybody.

Lonely Again

(A poem for the little hero Omran)

Here I am, lonely again, and crying alone.
I asked the moon, if he feels lonely?
He said I am warm from sun shine,
and happy with all the glowing stars.

Here I am, lonely again, but not crying.
I asked the death, if he likes his mission?
He said I am raising grief and flooding with blood.
Miserable for watching Omran by himself.

Colourless Dream

A sinner spirit forced me to sleep,
With my flesh bleeding my sins away,
On the pillow of my daily misery,
And cover myself with a dead body.

I close my eyes as my heart does too,
I dream with colourless dreams,
Believe me it was not a nightmare,
But a dark journey in my birth city.

Black dust from Baghdad's funerals,
White fog to hid the broken wings,
I looked for my childhood house,
I sought for the first love of my life.

I forgot to mention that I was blind,
I hear the moaning from the graveyard,
I made a vow to cry my blindness off,
And saw all the rainbow colors on her.

it started from her long golden hair,
all the way down to her pinky toe,
I asked for a kiss from her red lips,
so, I cloud stop the flow of blood.

I discovered I was wrong about red,
I saw some women lose their Virginity,
it created a pleasure into a crime scene.
two hearts died as their emotions were innocent.

some humans swallow each other's blood,
as if they were drinking soft drinks from a straw,
my age of one hundred years of dusty grieves,
it turned into a ten-year-old innocent child.

knowledgeable about everything around me,
I could define the gold digger from a
one night stand before going to one, as I
I have been betrayed and lost the one I loved.

I realized I was the last solider to Free Baghdad,
From all gunmen, and all the mindless terrorists,
With only one old gun within one magical bullet,
Not terrified, but I believe violence bring violence.

I shot my bullet to the black clouds in the real life,
To rain swords upon all the criminals in this world,
My dreams got the colors back when peace arose,
And I died happily and went flying up to the heaven.

The Crying Girl on the Border

On the Iraqi border,
there was a crying girl.
I cried for remembering
the days we had in the past

I asked her mother
"why is your daughter crying?"
with a soft voice, she responded,
"Because she wants her father".

I spread his ashes over
the border. Since then she
always thought her father
walked away from her

The doll she holds knows everything,
since it is the only being, she talks to
Sadly, the doll does not know
how to express to her about
her father's death

Will the Gate of Mesopotamia Open for Us?

Will we have to wait another?
century in front of the gate
without having the key to open it.

Will the nobles open the gate?
For us, with the keys, whom
almost went blind from crying tears

Will we get the chance to breathe?
the air of Babylon which can't be
Compare to and be found anywhere else

Will the people accept the fact that?
seeing us back to Baghdad to donate our souls
 to protect them from the unseen danger

Will they believe that our blood is always
more likely to be more drinkable than water
Precious for every single one of them

Will they realize that Iraq is not their mother
Only that she is and will be our mother too,
Who sadly pushed us away only to protect?
us and not to lose our lives that one day we will
Clean the mess that evil created in the past

Will they believe that we see the snow in
exile, black like the colour of the London clouds
but we are able to recognize the colour of the skies

In Baghdad they are blue just like the colour of
Tigris and Euphrates River

Will someone wake us up and give the key
so that our dreams can come true
instead of sleeping near
the gate for one more century?

If Santa Clause Was In...

The souls of dead angels who never liked the sound of weapons,
Came last night for a short visit, in between my dreams of Baghdad.

They asked me why Santa Clause can't come to visit us, since
He never protects us in the real world, or never appears in my dreams.

If Santa Clause was in Iraq, he would be blind from weeping
Since his late arrival, he wanted to give them a life during Christmas time.

If Santa Clause was in Syria, he would never forgive himself
Knowing that all the children waiting in tombs in the dying gardens.

If Santa Clause was in Palestine, he would be the only soul to witness
Watching children search between their destroyed homes to receive their gifts.

If Santa Clause was in Africa, he would probably be dead from
watching children with minds to kill their parents or even their childhood friends.

I got nothing to say to them, but I promised them that
   I will talk to him,
Sadly, they never knew that he doesn't exist in the
   real world or even in our dreams.

One of them asked me why their children are happier
   with their gifts,
While us, we celebrate Christmas with no gifts but
   with a joy of our parents.

My Childhood

My teacher said that she lost her childhood,
once she knew that Santa Claus was not real.

She asked me how I lost my childhood,
I answered her with a heart breaking into tears

I lost my childhood once I knew that my friends,
Were dead from plastic guns that killed them all.

I tried to save their lives, I knocked on their doors,
No one answered, but the doors opened to show me their graves.

The Second World War ended years ago, but their
Mothers witnessed it, as proof that they're blind now.

I looked up at the middle of the skies, to watch their souls
As doves who don't like the sounds horrifying, weapons.

Water Versus Wine

When
I drink
water
my
words
become
clear pictures and happy fantasies
when
I drink
wine
my
words
become
dark poems and sad realities

Ahmad Al-Khatat was born in Baghdad, Iraq. He has been published in several press publications and anthologies all over the world and has poems translated in several languages. His previously published poetry books *The Bleeding Heart Poet*, *Love On The War's Frontline*, and *Gas Chamber* are available online. You can follow Ahmad online at:

facebook.com/Bleedingheartpoet

www.ingramcontent.com/pod-product-compliance
Lightning Source LLC
Chambersburg PA
CBHW030104100526
44591CB00008B/267